SCENES OF EVERYDAY LIFE

DUTCH GENRE PAINTINGS FROM THE MAURITSHUIS

CHRISTOPHER BROWN

ASHMOLEAN MUSEUM
OXFORD

Published to coincide with the loan exhibition to the
ASHMOLEAN MUSEUM 9 November 1999 to 9 January 2000

ISBN 1 85444 126 4

British Library Cataloguing in Publications Data:
A catalogue record of this book is available from the British Library

Designed and typeset in Van Dijck by Tim Harvey

Printed and bound in Great Britain by BAS Printers 1999

The ASHMOLEAN MUSEUM would like to acknowledge the generous help of Johnny van Haeften Ltd., The Artemis Group, Colnaghi, Hall and Knight Ltd., Otto Naumann Ltd. (New York) and the Dutch Embassy in London towards the expenses of this exhibition.

Cover illustration: GERARD TER BORCH : *Woman writing a letter* (PLATE 18)

PREFACE

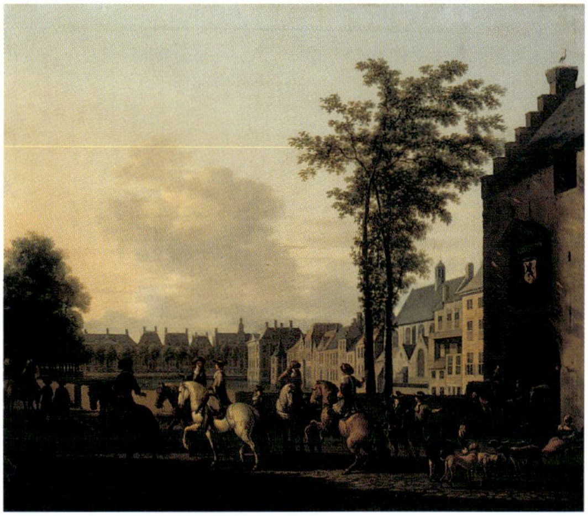

Gerrit Berckheyde : *The Hofvijver in The Hague with a view of the Mauritshuis*
Canvas, 58 × 68.5 cm.
Signed : gerret: Berck Heijde

The Royal Cabinet of Paintings Mauritshuis in The Hague is, after the Rijksmuseum, the most important collection of Dutch 17th-century paintings in The Netherlands, known throughout the world for masterpieces which include Rembrandt's Anatomy Lesson of Dr Tulp and Vermeer's View of Delft.

The collection is housed in one of the finest classical buildings in the country which was built as a town palace for Johan Maurits, Count of Nassau-Siegen and takes its name from its first owner. As can be seen in this view by Gerrit Berckheyde, it stands on the edge of the Hofvijver, part of the castle-moat surrounding the mediaeval castle of the counts of Holland.

The Mauritshuis's collection represents all the varied types of painting made during the Golden Age, portraiture, still life, marines, landscapes, topographical views, church interiors and genre paintings. Its group of the last type, genre paintings, is particularly strong and in the paintings included in this exhibition, the remarkable range and variety of these scenes based on the everyday lives of the Dutch of the seventeenth century are displayed.

The Mauritshuis is pleased to present this small but choice selection of its holdings in recognition of the longstanding excellent relations with British museums in general and with Christopher Brown, Director of the Ashmolean Museum in Oxford, in particular.

Frederik J. Duparc, *Director, Mauritshuis*

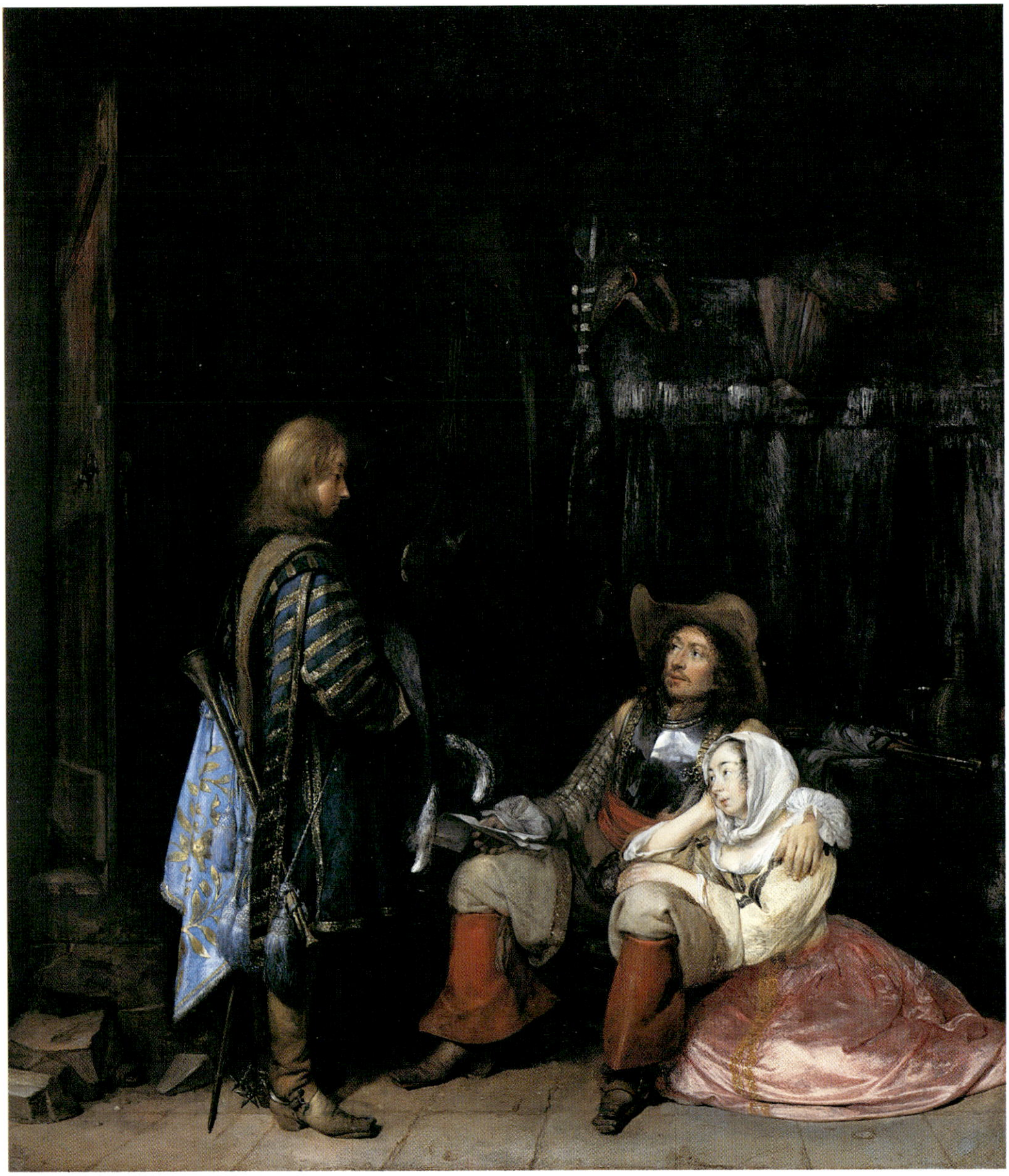

PLATE I

GERARD TER BORCH : *Unwelcome News*

Panel, 66.7 × 59.5 cm.

Signed, GTB (in monogram) 1653

SCENES OF EVERYDAY LIFE: DUTCH GENRE PAINTING OF THE 17TH CENTURY

THE Dutch Republic of the 17th century was a new society, a society born of religious conflict and a war of independence, of large-scale immigration and rapid urbanization. It is unsurprising, therefore, that it was the birthplace of a new art, an art which was largely non-religious and celebrated the physical appearance of the country and its inhabitants, delighting in the details of their daily lives. This was truly a Golden Age of portraiture and landscape but the type of painting which most strongly characterises this new art is genre painting, the representation of scenes from everyday life. The mothers and children of Vermeer and Pieter de Hooch, the soldiers and lovers of Gerard ter Borch (PLATE 1) and Gabriel Metsu, the kitchenmaids and musicians of Nicolaes Maes and Gerrit Dou, the farmers and villagers of Isack and Adriaen van Ostade (PLATE 2) and the skaters of Aert van der Neer are all shown going about their daily lives in an unforced and entirely natural manner. For the first time in European art ordinary lives became an important subject for painters.

In its modern sense 'genre' is a very broad term and it comes as no surprise to discover that it was unknown in the seventeenth century. The French word, literally meaning 'kind' or 'sort', was first applied to a wide range of paintings showing scenes from everyday life in 18th-century France. In the 17th century the Dutch used a variety of words to describe many of the subjects today subsumed within the catch-all of genre. A scene depicting elegantly dressed young men and women in an interior eating, drinking, playing musical instruments and flirting as painted by Willem Buytewech and Dirk Hals (PLATE 3) was known as a *geselschapje* or a *conversatie*, while an outdoor scene of the same type was a *buitenpartij*. A painting of soldiers in their guardroom was a *cortegaerdje* and Roman street scenes were known by the Italian term *bamboccianti*. Each of these subjects had its own pictorial tradition and the word which comes closest to covering them all was *beeldeken*, which simply means a painting with small figures.

The Dutch wrote less about their art than the Italians but in the relatively few theoretical discussions of painting in 17th-century Holland there are almost no accounts of genre painting. If mentioned at all, it is condemned as unworthy and Dutch painters are urged to treat elevated subjects from the Bible and mythology in a classicising manner. Genre painting is a genuinely popular art, not based on theory but developing in response to the demands of a vigorous art

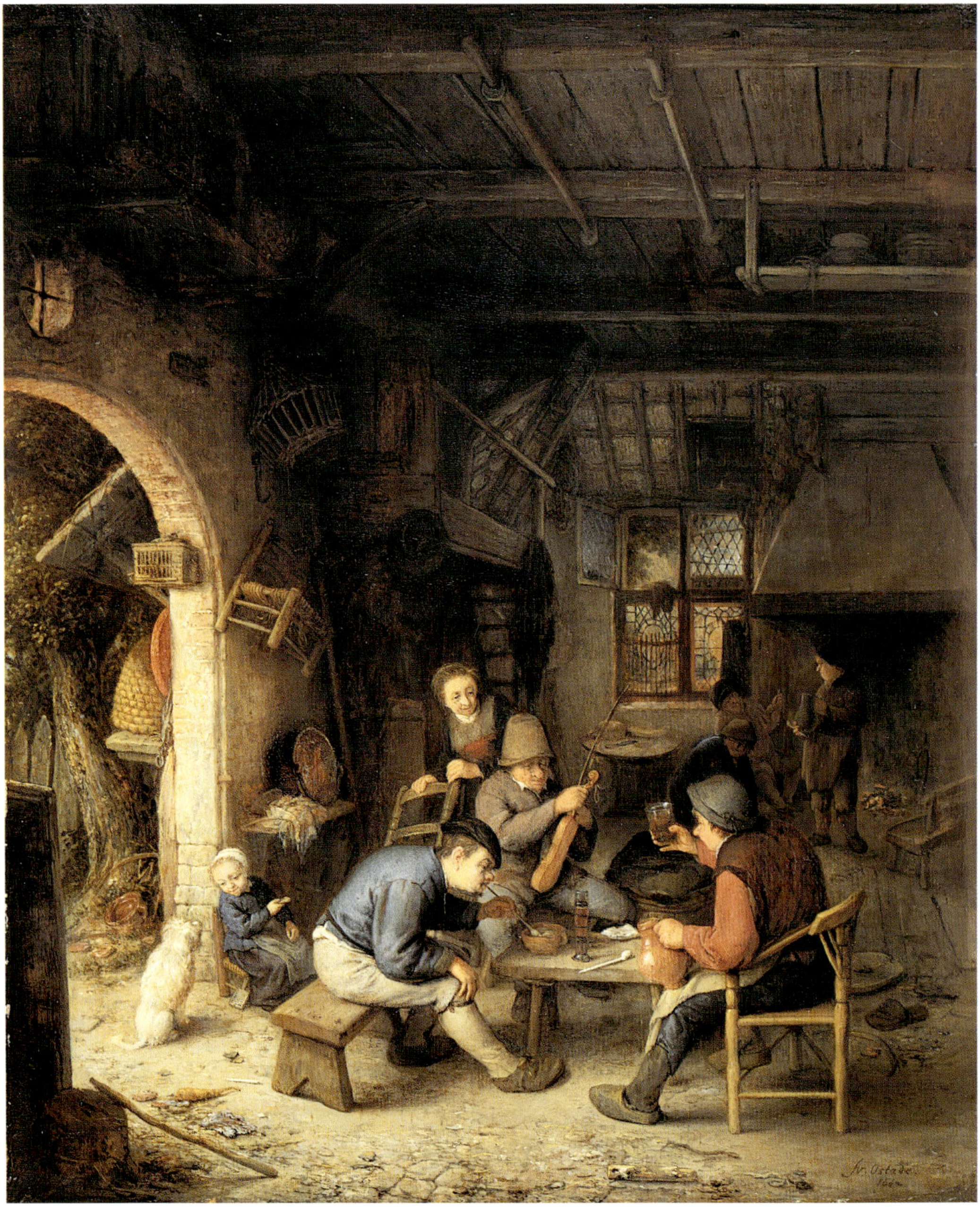

PLATE 2
ADRIAEN VAN OSTADE : *Peasants in an Inn*
Panel, 47 × 39 cm.
Signed and dated : Av. Ostade 1662

market, where for the first time people of relatively modest means were able to buy paintings. This was a phenomenon often commented upon by foreign visitors. Visiting the Rotterdam fair in 1641 John Evelyn found it "so furnished with pictures (especially landscips and drolleries [by which he meant scenes of country life], as they call these clownish representations) as I was amaz'd . . . 'tis an ordinary thing to find a common farmer lay out two or three thousand pounds in this commodity, their houses are full of them, and they vend them at their kermesses to very great gains." The English traveller Peter Mundy noted "all in general striving to adorn their houses, especially the outer or street room, with costly pieces, butchers and bakers not much inferior in their shops which are fairly set forth, yea many times blacksmiths, cobblers etc. will have some picture or other by their forge and in their stalls."

This new public demanded paintings which were modestly priced and showed familiar subjects. Few collectors were classically educated and the majority had little desire to have scenes from Roman history or Greek mythology on their walls. They preferred Dutch landscapes, topographical views of their town, interiors of the churches in which they worshipped and scenes of everyday life. In a society experiencing great changes caused by rapid economic growth and urbanization such paintings may well have appealed to nostalgic sentiments. Many city-dwellers had moved from the country or were the first generation to be born in the cities of the Republic and the continuing demand for scenes of country life may reflect a longing for a simpler existence.

The beginnings of genre painting lie in the calendar illustrations showing the activities of the month in late medieval prayerbooks and in scenes of town and country life tucked into the backgrounds of religious paintings. It was in Antwerp in the mid-16th century that paintings of everyday activities free of any religious connotations were first made, a development closely associated with the studio of

PLATE 3
DIRK HALS : *Merry Company*
Panel, 30 × 51.5 cm.
Signed and dated : D Hals 1635

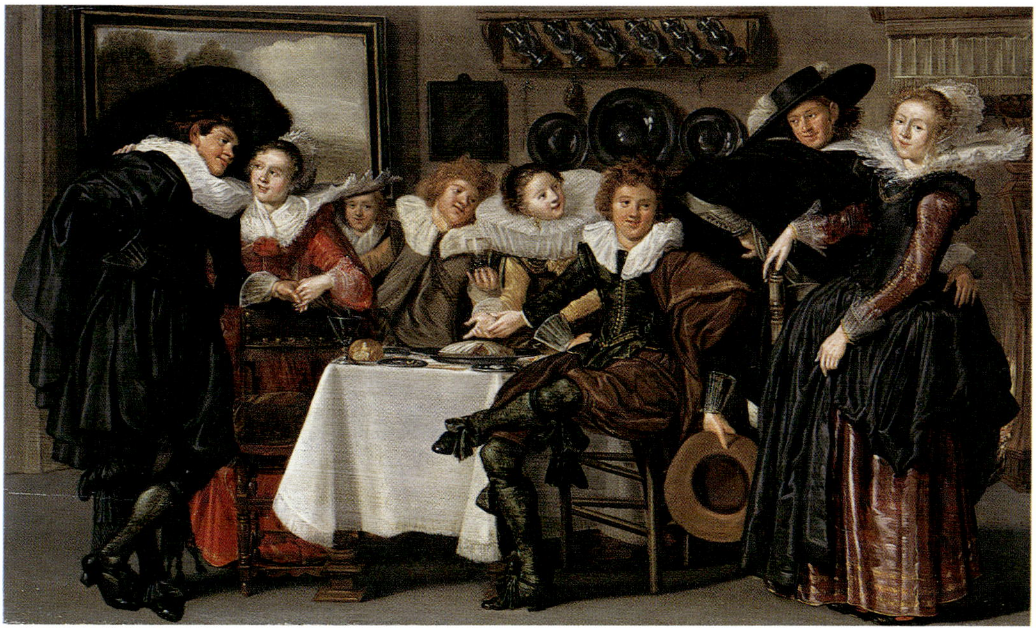

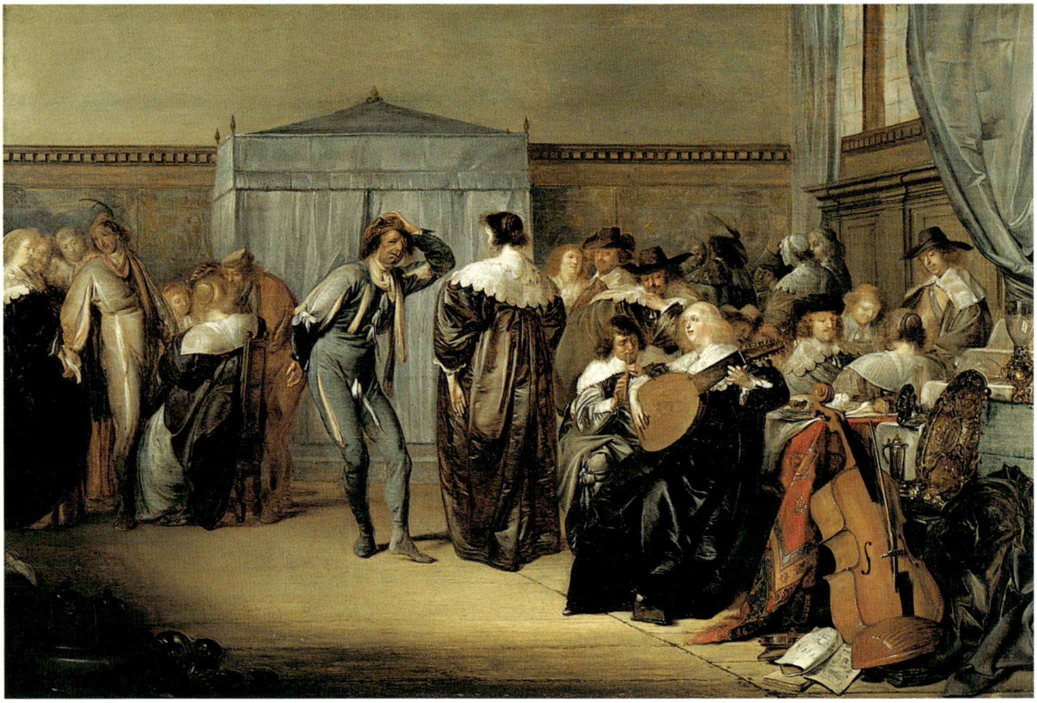

PLATE 4
PIETER CODDE :
Festivity with masked dancers
Panel, 50 × 76.5 cm.
Signed and dated :
Pcodde Ao 1636

Pieter Bruegel the Elder. In his engravings of Spring and Summer, which are in the tradition of the illuminated calendar pages, the real subject is the work of the muscular gardeners and harvesters. Bruegel designed prints of skaters on the ice in Antwerp, peasant revels and scenes from popular dramas. He also painted scenes of the months and naturalistic compendia of Netherlandish proverbs and children's games. His work, widely circulated in the form of engravings, was immensely influential. A number of Antwerp painters familiar with Bruegel's innovations moved to the north, and to Amsterdam in particular, as a consequence of the war between Spain and the Dutch Republic. These ideas then took strong root in the northern Netherlands.

Amsterdam, the commercial and financial heart of the Dutch Republic, occupies a central position in the history of Dutch genre painting: it provided much of the initial impetus and subsequently acted as a magnet for talented provincial artists anxious to explore its large market. It was in Amsterdam that David Vinckboons, whose painter father had moved from Antwerp, developed Flemish peasant subjects. Pieter Codde (PLATE 4) and Willem Duyster (PLATE 5) also lived and worked in the city. Codde was a portraitist as well as a painter of small, highly finished genre scenes, which often show elegantly dressed figures eating, drinking and cardplaying; Duyster

PLATE 5
WILLEM CORNELISZ. DUYSTER : *An Officer*
Panel, 40 × 31.5 cm.

had a particular interest in barrack-room scenes and also painted interiors similar to those of Codde and his Amsterdam brother-in-law Simon Kick. This group of painters of *cortegaerdjes* and interiors was principally active in the 1620s and 1630s. Amsterdam also attracted provincial painters throughout the seventeenth century. It was by

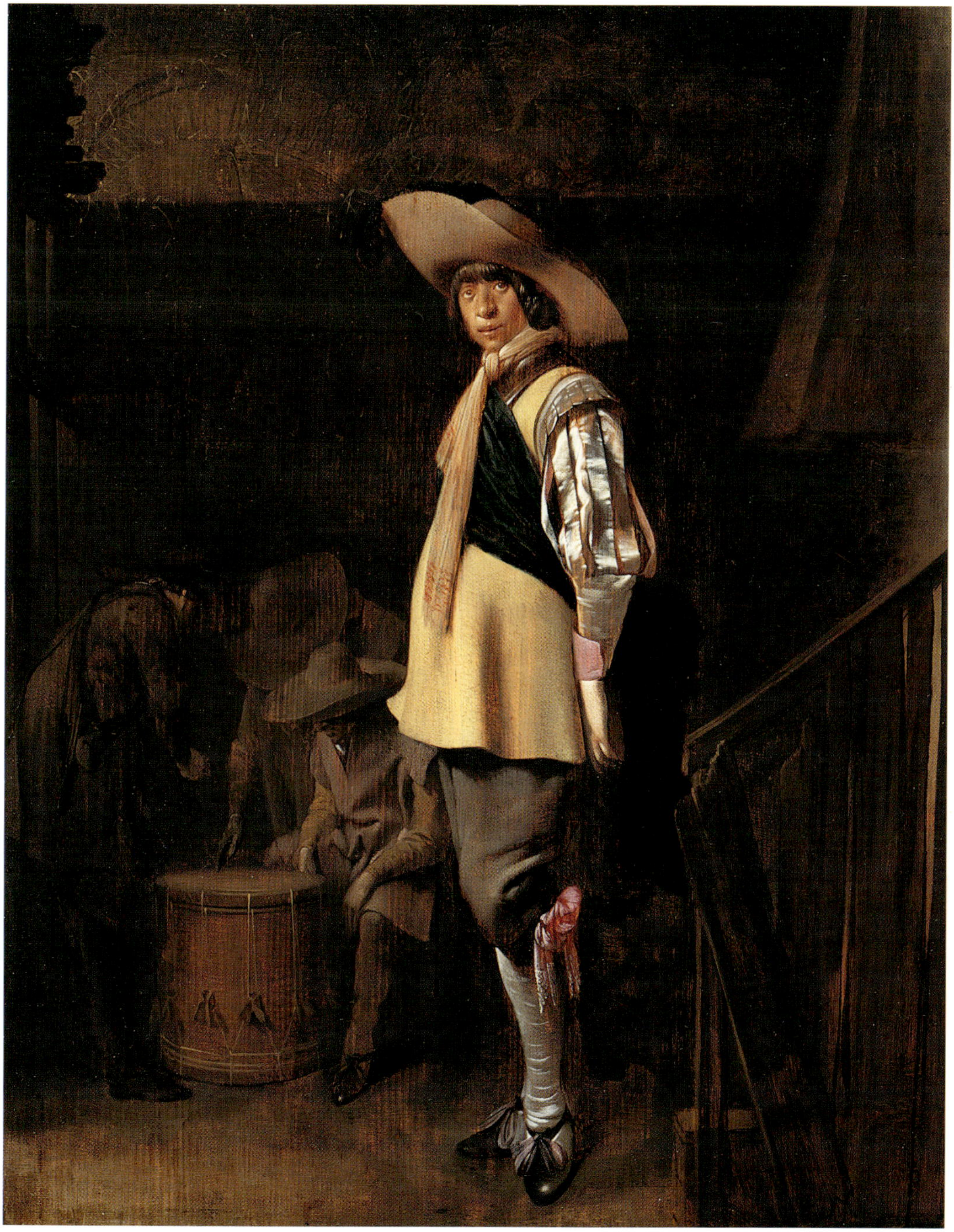

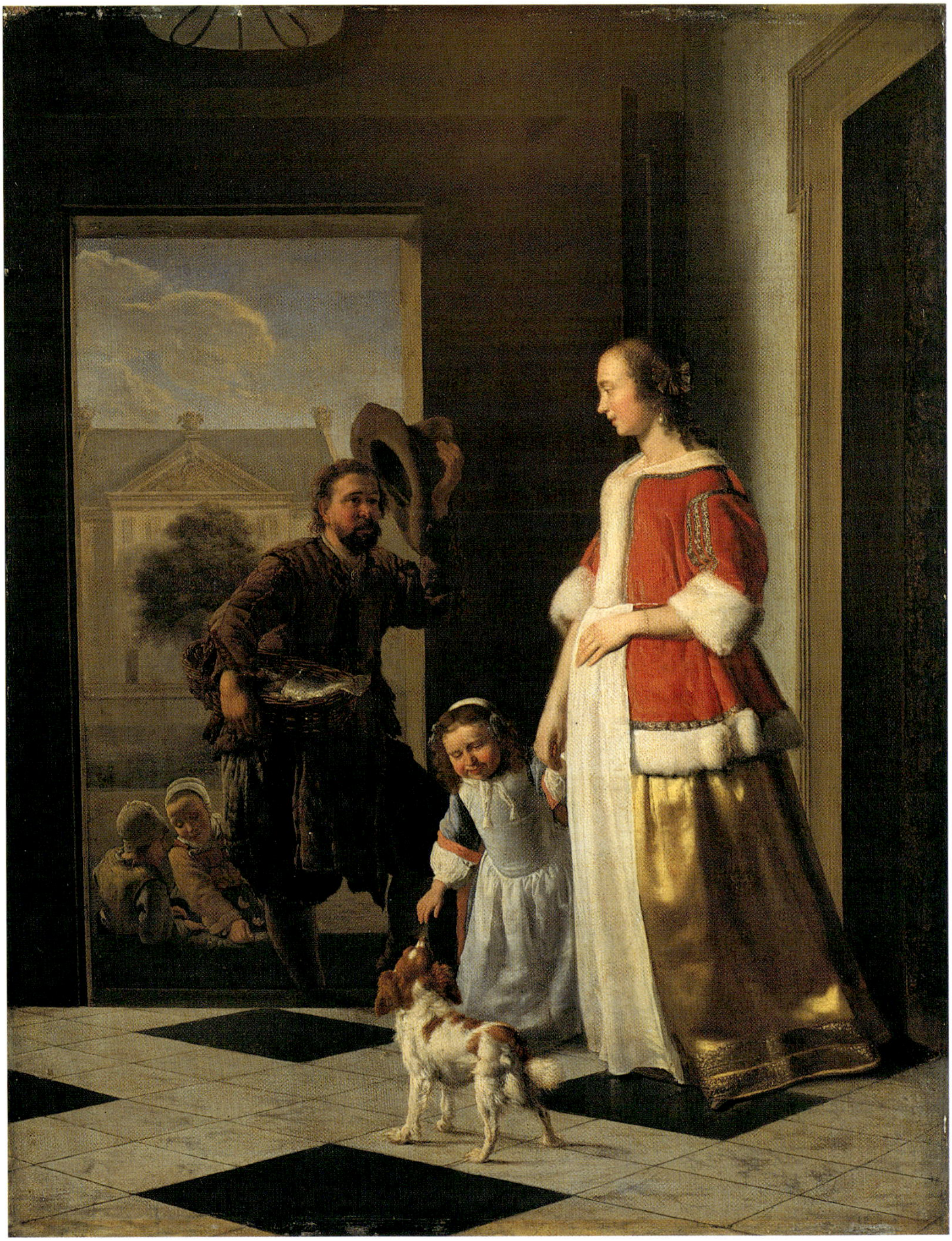

PLATE 6
JACOB OCHTERVELT :
The Fishmonger
Canvas, 55.5 × 44 cm.

far the largest city in the Netherlands and had a population which was wealthier and more adventurous in its tastes than anywhere else. It possessed a lively art market with enterprising dealers and regular auctions of Italian, French and Flemish as well as Dutch paintings. A particularly important group of genre painters was working there in the thirty years after 1650. Gabriel Metsu moved to Amsterdam from Leiden in the 1650s; Pieter de Hooch had arrived from Delft by 1661; and Jacob Ochtervelt (PLATE 6) had come from Rotterdam by 1674.

Haarlem, being a relatively small provincial town (with a population of only 40,000 in 1622) whose principal industries were brewing and weaving, had a quite different character. It possessed a prosperous regent (or governing) class, depicted in Frans Hals' group portraits, and a large community of Flemish immigrants. The town is particularly associated in the early 17th century with the development of the 'merry company' scene. Among its most accomplished exponents were Dirk Hals, the younger brother of Frans, and Esaias van de Velde, who moved to The Hague in 1618. A third Haarlem painter of 'merry company' scenes and *cortegaerdjes*, Hendrick Pot, worked for Charles I in London and finally moved to Amsterdam in about 1650. The painters Jan Molenaer (PLATES 7–11) and Judith Leyster, who married in 1636, both reveal the influence of Frans Hals in their slashing brushstrokes and bright palettes. They painted genre scenes almost exclusively: Molenaer specialised in interiors with young people and children. Frans Hals is also said to have been the master of Adriaen van Ostade, who enjoyed a long and prolific career as a painter of country life in Haarlem. Such scenes are particularly associated with Haarlem in the work not only of Adriaen van Ostade but also of his short-lived brother Isack and his pupil

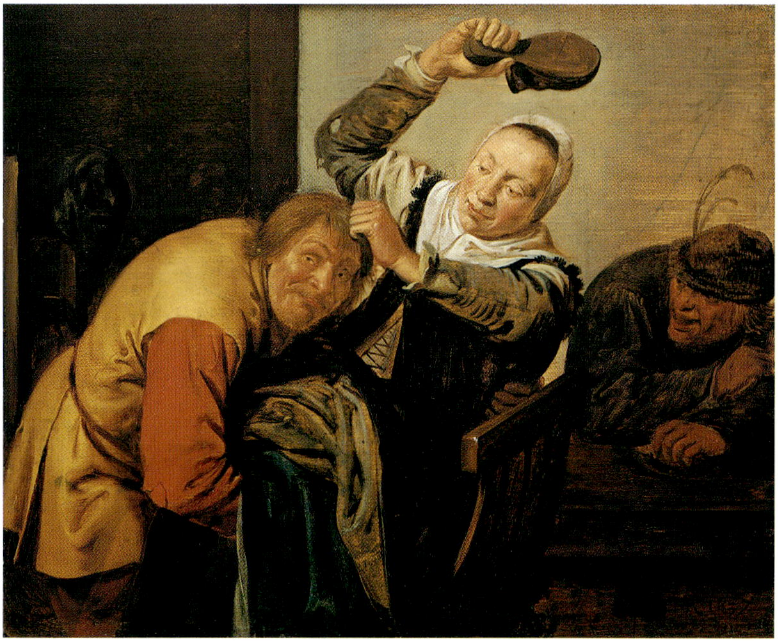

PLATE 7
JAN MIENSE MOLENAER : *The Five Senses : Touch*
Panel, 19.5 × 24.2 cm.
Signed and dated : IMR 1637

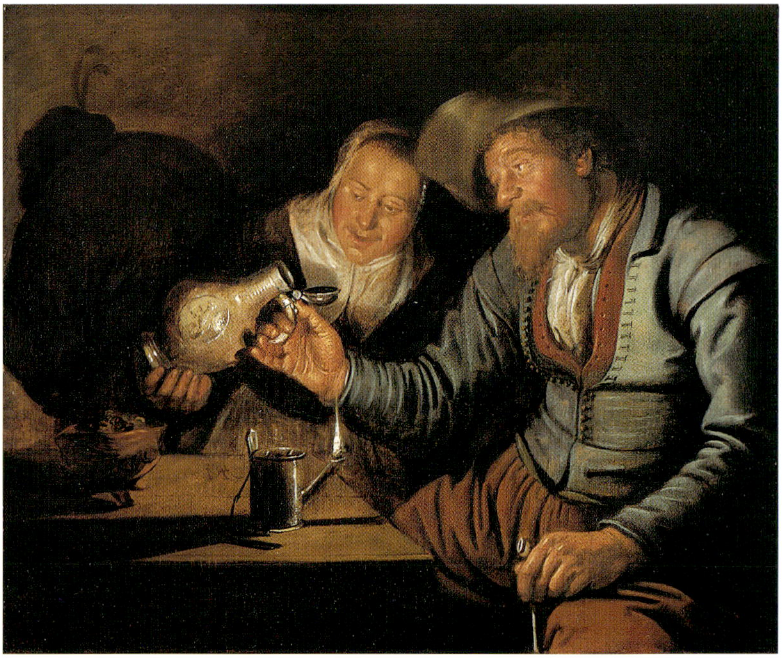

PLATE 8
JAN MIENSE MOLENAER : *The Five Senses : Sight*
Panel, 19.6 × 23.9 cm.
Signed : IMR

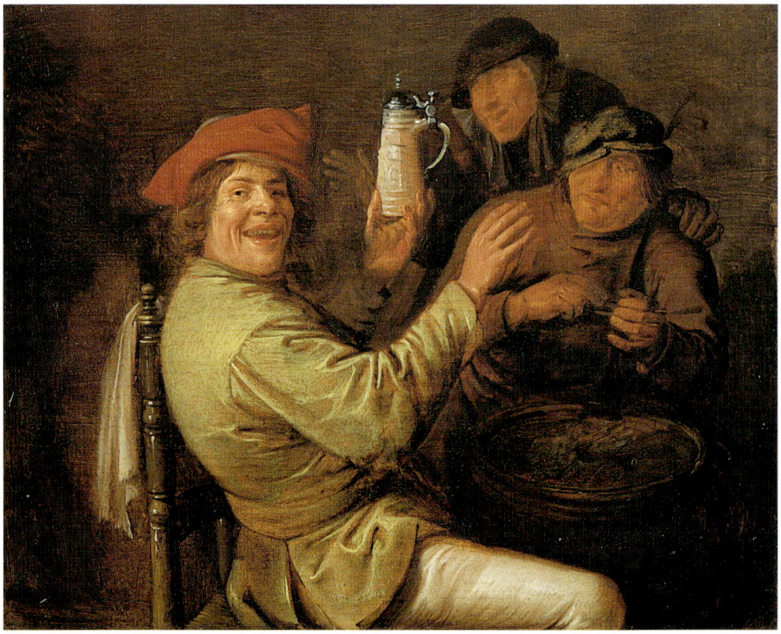

PLATE 9
JAN MIENSE MOLENAER : *The Five Senses : Sound*
Panel, 19.4 × 24.2 cm.

Cornelis Dusart. It was also from Haarlem that Pieter van Laer set out for Rome, where he gave his Italian nickname 'Il Bamboccio' to an entirely new type of genre painting, the Roman street scene.

As a huge centre for textile manufacture, Leiden was the largest industrial town in the Republic and the seat of its oldest and most

PLATE 10
JAN MIENSE MOLENAER : *The Five Senses : Smell*
Panel, 19.5 × 24.3 cm.

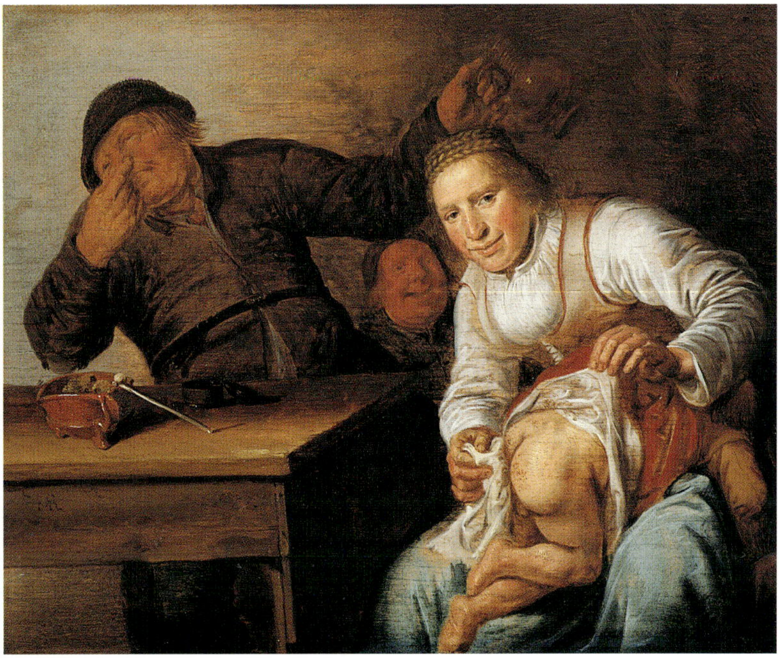

PLATE 11
JAN MIENSE MOLENAER : *The Five Senses : Taste*
Panel, 19.6 × 24.1 cm.

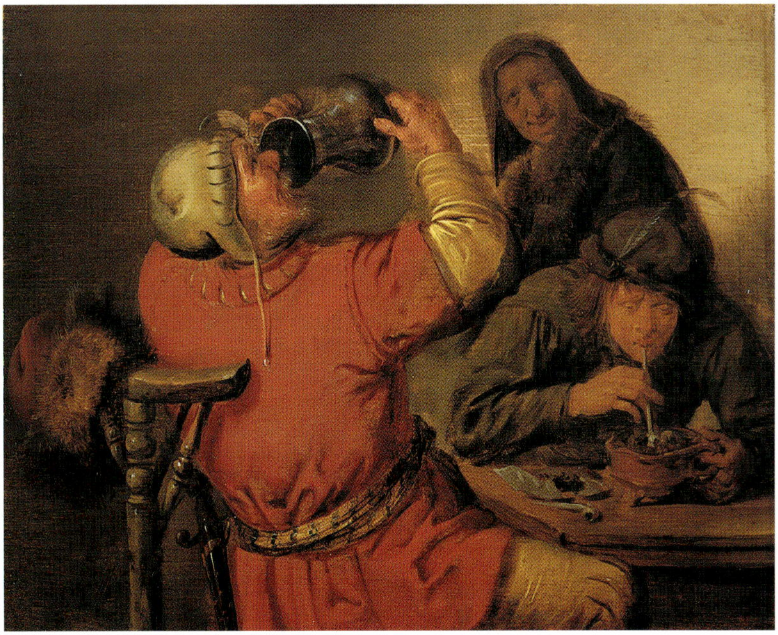

distinguished university. In terms of genre painting, Leiden's distinct personality was created by the town's leading painter, Gerrit Dou (PLATE 12). He had a wide range of original and often highly sophisticated subject-matter : complicated allegories as well as interiors with musicians and mothers and children, single figures and

PLATE 12
GERARD DOU : *Young woman holding a lamp*
Panel, 19 × 14 cm.

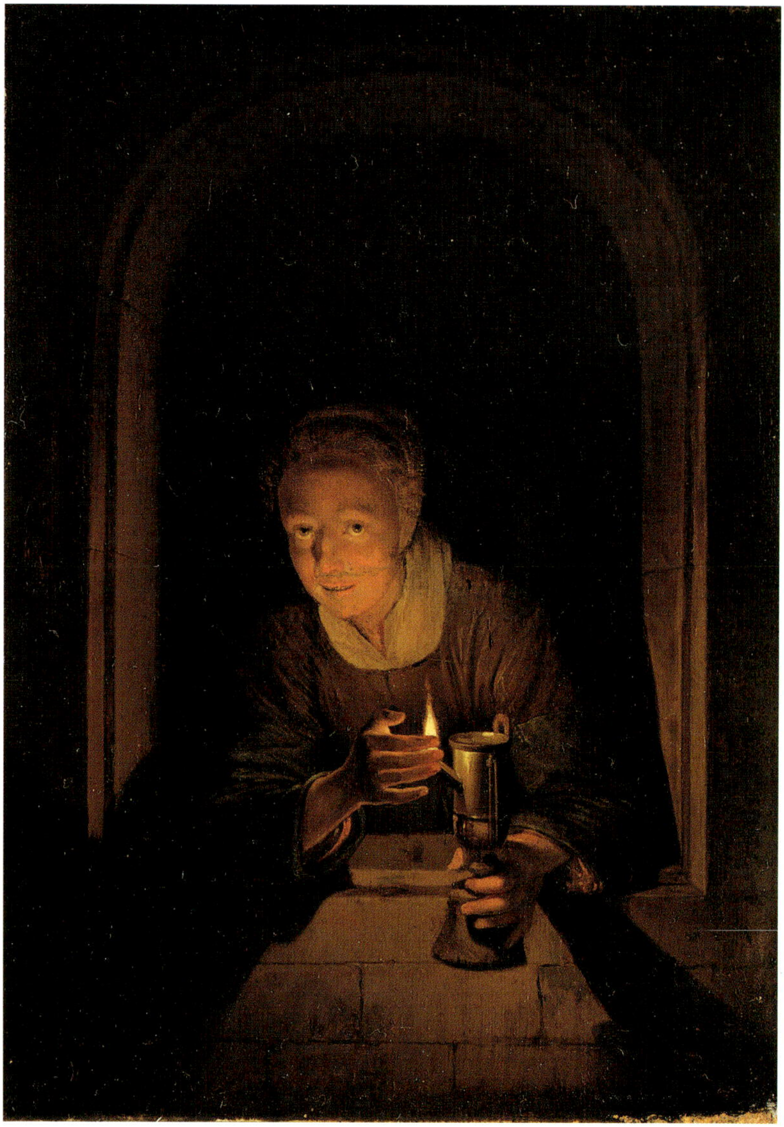

the so-called 'niche' paintings, in which domestic interiors and shops are seen through an open window. Dou's highly finished technique was adopted by his followers, notably Frans van Mieris (PLATE 13), whom he is said to have called "the Prince of my pupils", and Godfried Schalcken (PLATES 14, 23). From this meticulous style they are collectively known as *fijnschilders*. Both Van Mieris and Schalcken, like Dou, were highly successful artists with a Europe-wide reputation. The *fijnschilder* tradition in Leiden was continued into the 18th century by Frans van Mieris' sons, Jan and Willem and by his grandson, Frans the Younger. Metsu (PLATE 15) is also said to have been a pupil of Dou but his work does not belong to the *fijnschilder* tradition: his open brushwork suggests a Flemish influence. He had left Leiden for Amsterdam by 1657.

Up until 1650 Delft, a city whose political and economic Golden Age had been in the 16th century, was a modest centre for painting, best known for the portraits of Mierevelt. In 1650 Carel Fabritius settled in Delft ; two years later Pieter de Hooch is first recorded there ; and 1656 is the earliest date on a painting by Jan Vermeer, who had been born in the town. Jan Steen and Gerard ter Borch both visited the town during that eventful decade. These artists do not strictly constitute a school of painting but they did share certain preoccupations – the rendition of light and its daytime effects, the expressive possibilities of space, and certain simple, domestic

PLATE 13
FRANS VAN MIERIS THE ELDER : *Teasing the pet*
Panel, 27.5 × 20 cm.
Signed and dated : Fv Mieris Ao 1660

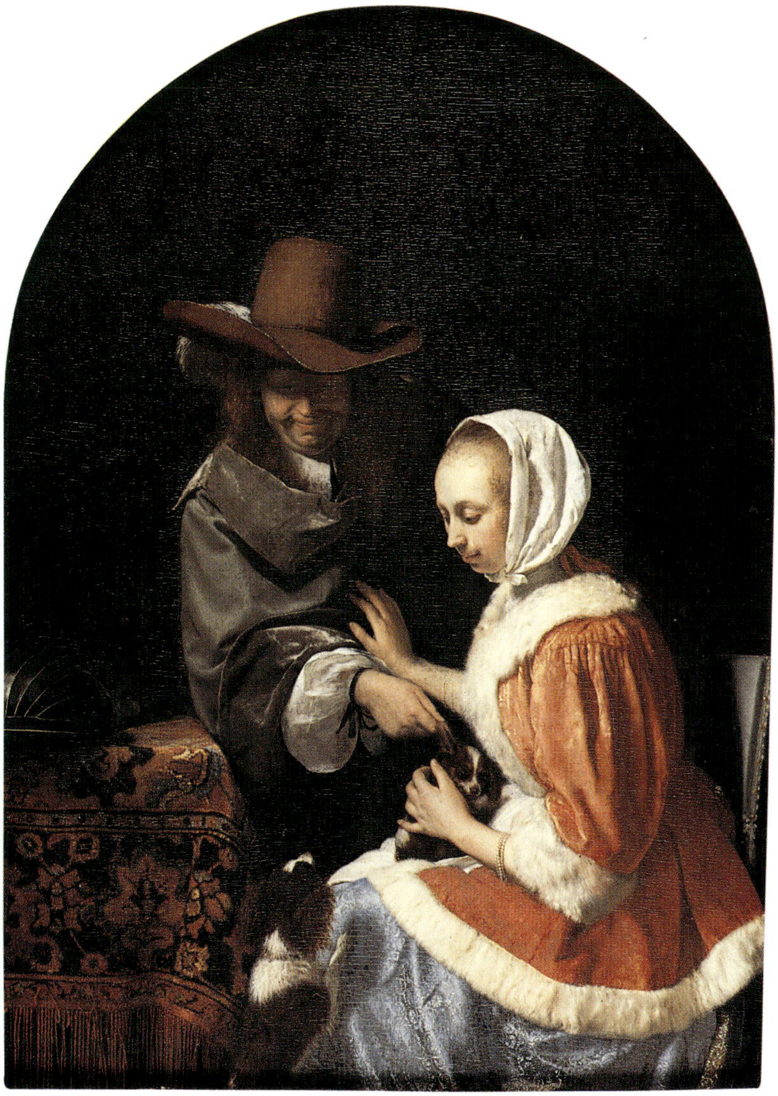

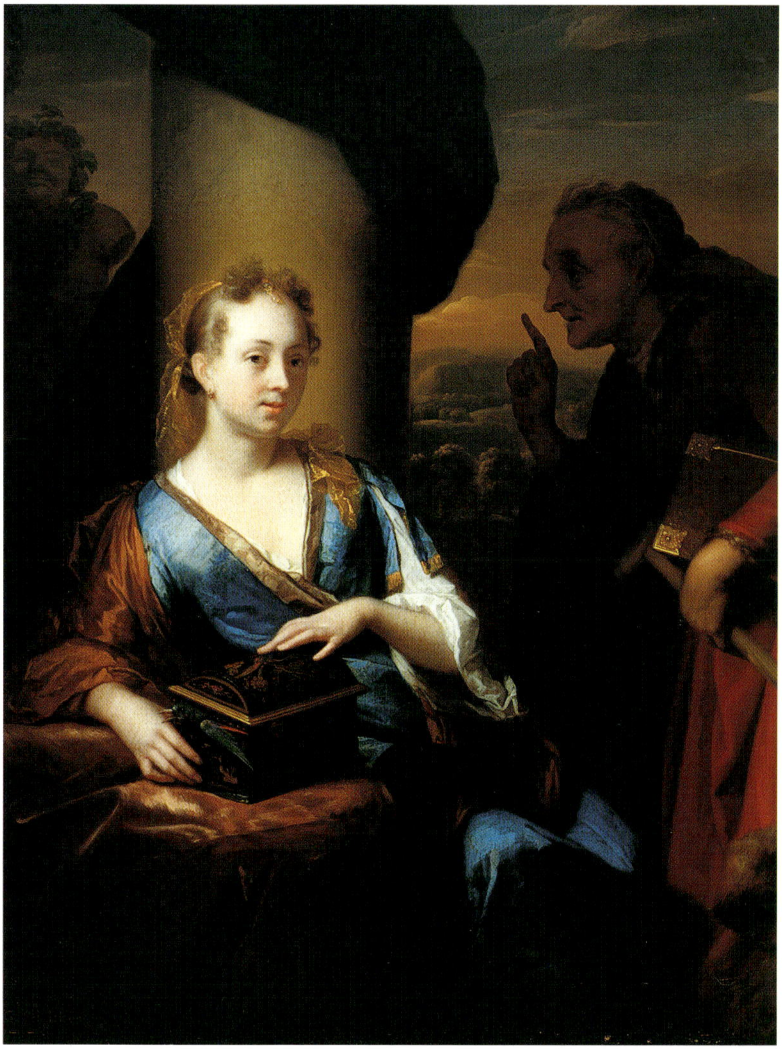

PLATE 14
GODFRIED SCHALCKEN : *The wasted lesson in morals*
Panel, 35 × 28.5 cm.
Signed : G. Schalcken

This painting and its pair (PLATE 23) together tell a story of the loss of innocence. In the 17th century a locked casket was often employed as a symbol of a young woman's virginity. In the first scene an elderly woman admonishes the young woman with a wagging finger not to open the casket. Her words, however, go unheeded. She does open the casket and in the second painting, the consequences of her recklessness can be seen. A doctor examines her urine, a common method of determining pregnancy. The young woman, discovering that she is pregnant, weeps in the background. The boy on the right makes a crude gesture which further underlines the reason for her plight. Both the old woman and the doctor are mocked and Schalcken's tone is one of amusement at the inevitability of the young woman's actions rather than high-minded moral condemnation.

subjects. Nicolaes Maes (PLATE 16) had been a pupil with Fabritius in Rembrandt's Amsterdam studio. He returned to his native Dordrecht, a busy port at the mouth of the River Maas, in the second half of the 1650s and painted a number of small domestic interiors which, while employing a dark palette, share many of the characteristics of Delft paintings. After 1660 Maes confined himself to portraiture.

The Hague took its lead from the patronage of the house of Orange, whose taste was for a Flemish-influenced classicism. A number of artists were attracted there including Caspar Netscher, who had been a pupil of ter Borch, Adriaen van de Venne and the Utrecht painter Gerard Honthorst. Like the other leading Utrecht artists Hendrick ter Brugghen and Dirk van Baburen, Honthorst had

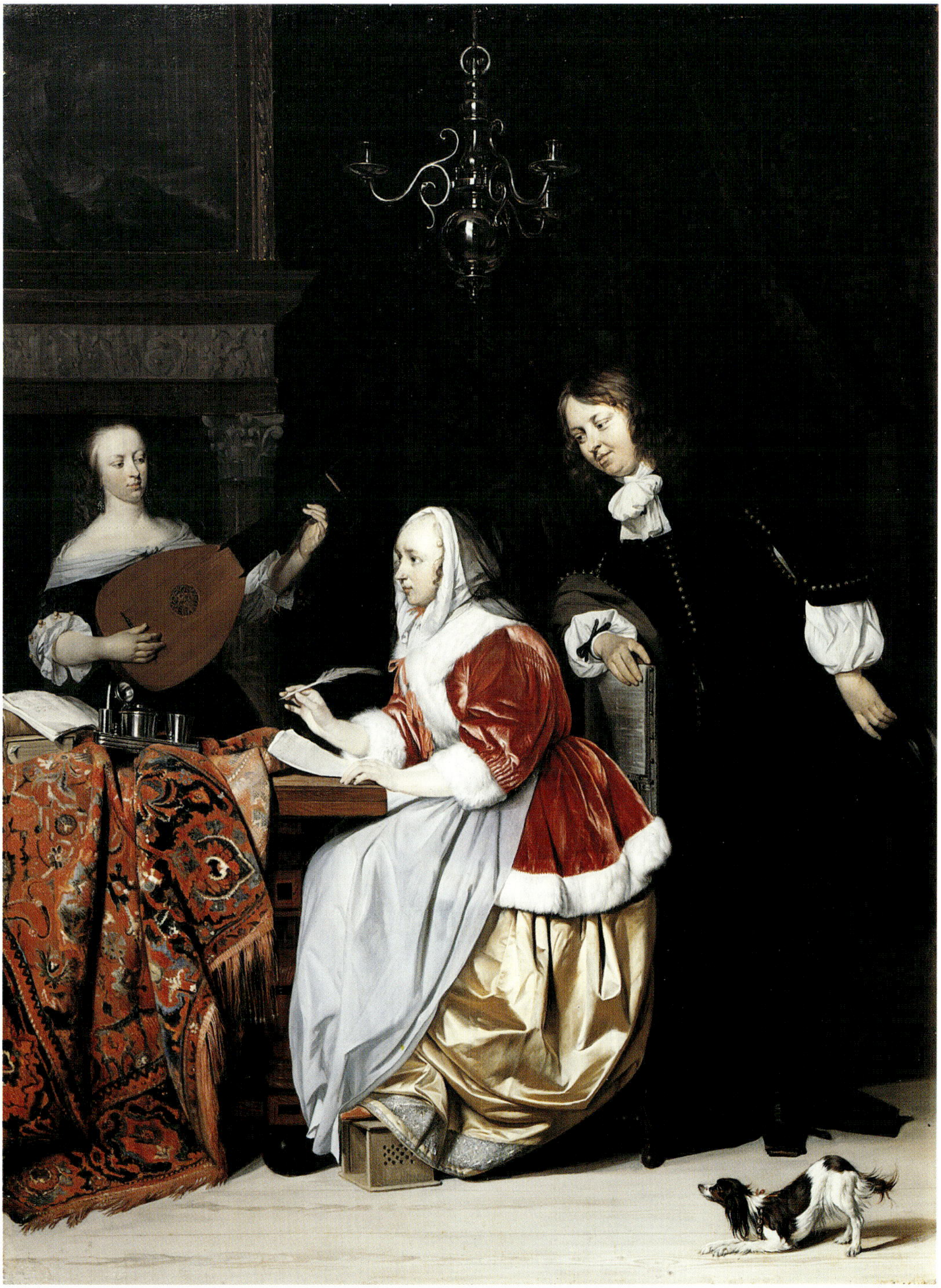

PLATE 15 GABRIEL METSU : *A Young Woman composing music*
Panel, 57.8 × 43.5 cm.
Signed : G Metsu

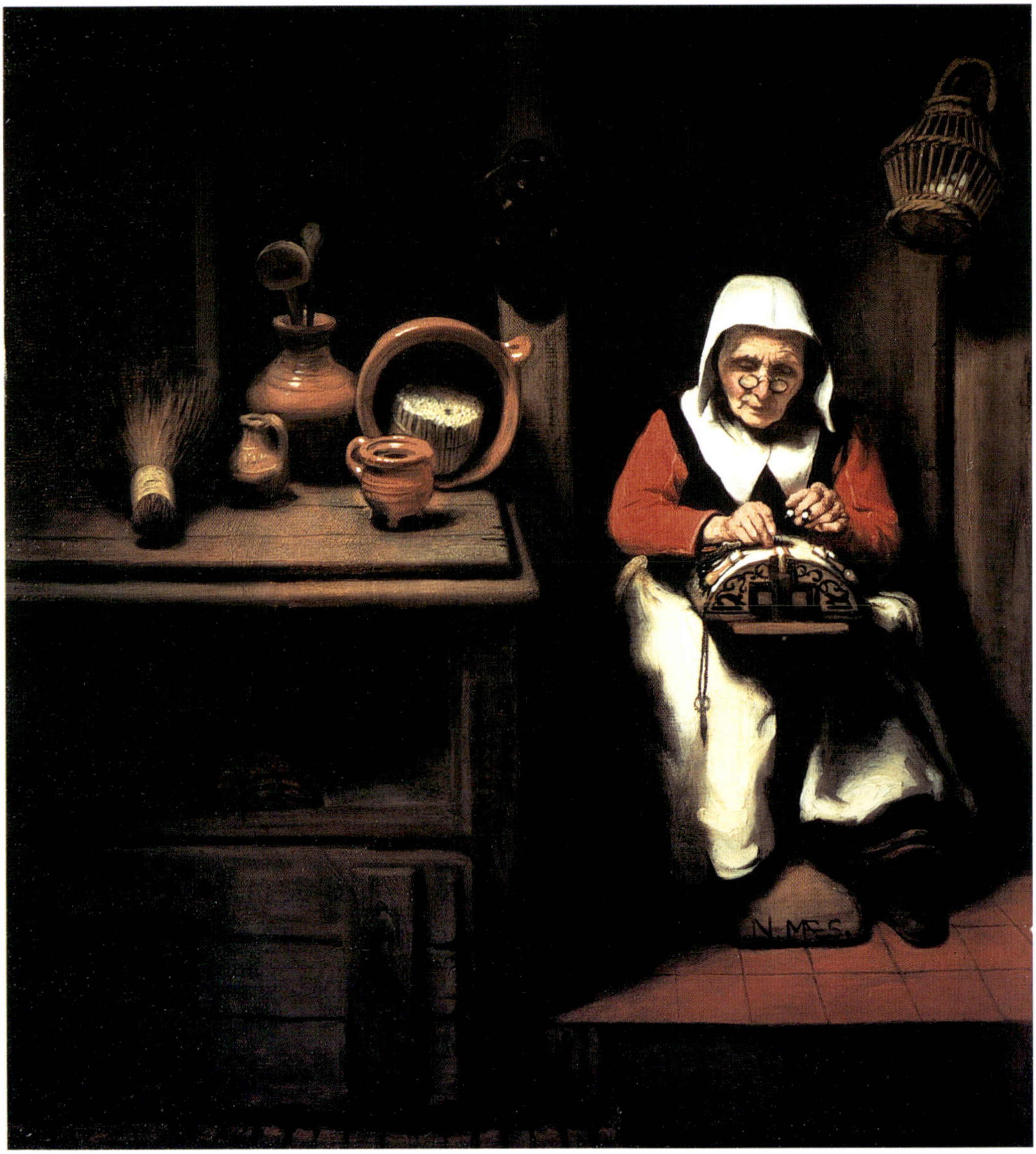

PLATE 16
NICOLAES MAES : *The Old Lace-maker*
Canvas, 37.5 × 35 cm.

travelled to Italy after his training and once there had been overwhelmed by the revolution in painting brought about by Caravaggio. On their return to Utrecht the three young artists painted musical parties, single musicians and drinkers on a large scale, with half-length figures illuminated by powerful contrasts of light and dark. These Utrecht painters treat such genre subjects with a rich palette and subtle technique but they remain outside the main currents of Dutch genre painting. Both ter Brugghen and Baburen died in the 1620s, while Honthorst turned increasingly towards classicising history painting and portraiture in his later, and highly successful, years spent both in Utrecht and The Hague, where he was court painter to the Prince of Orange.

Painters who lived in the same town often had a community of interest or enjoyed an exchange of ideas rather than forming a local school of painting in the Italian sense. Some were drawn to Amsterdam but others moved from town to town for a variety of personal and financial reasons. Jan Steen (PLATE 17) seems to have been constantly on the move: born in Leiden, he is known to have lived in Haarlem, The Hague, Warmond and Delft. Perhaps this provides some explanation for the fascinating variety of Steen's subject-matter and styles. Gerard ter Borch (PLATE 18), after extensive travels in Europe and stays in Amsterdam and Kampen,

PLATE 17
JAN STEEN : *Girl eating oysters*
Panel, 20.5 × 14.5 cm.
Signed : IS

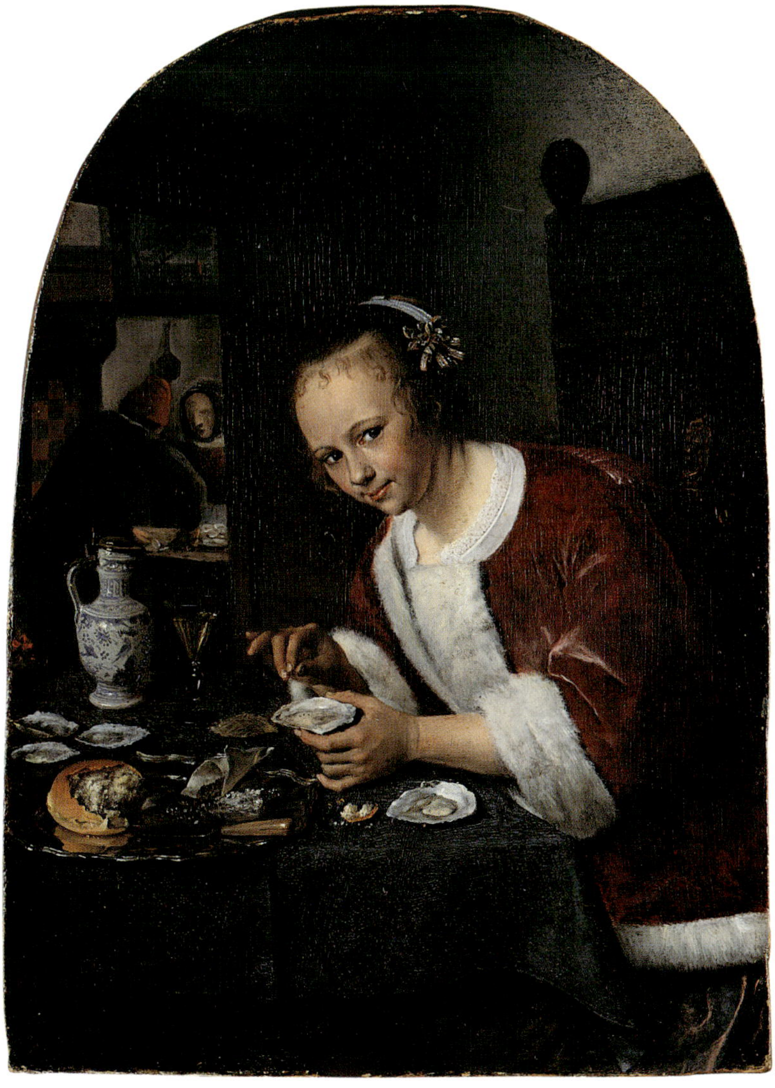

settled in the small provincial town of Deventer in his native province of Overijssel and was assimilated into its regent class. It was in Deventer that he developed the small-scale genre scenes which are so rich in descriptive detail and psychological nuance.

Dutch genre paintings show everyday life and yet are not purely descriptive. They are not snapshots of daily life taken at random, but carefully constructed accounts of the reality which the painters saw around them. Many of the earliest genre paintings were painted in the tradition of 16th century print series showing, for example, the Seasons, the Five Senses and the Virtues and Vices. An idea which in a 16th-century print had been represented by a female allegorical figure was now represented by a familiar scene from everyday life. A particularly striking example is the sense of smell, which was shown in a 16th-century print as a young woman in classical dress smelling the scent of a bouquet of flowers and by Jan Molenaer (PLATE 10) as a father recoiling from the smell of his baby's bottom. Clearly a major shift has taken place : in the print it is the allegorical representation of the sense which takes first place, whereas in the Molenaer the representation of the sense is simply a convenient opportunity to show an amusing scene from life.

The 'merry company' scenes of Dirk Hals and his Haarlem contemporaries show young people enjoying themselves drinking, smoking, playing music and flirting. When these scenes were engraved, an inscription was added stressing the moral danger in which these young people were placing themselves. Did Hals himself mean to condemn their foolishness and self-indulgence or was this inscription added by the publisher to justify the portraying of these riotous scenes ? While it is impossible to be sure, it is unlikely that genre paintings were used to point morals of this kind. Genre paintings are not sermons, religious tracts or moral emblems. Rather, they are precisely what they seem to be, carefully chosen and constructed accounts of everyday life, which were valued by contemporaries for the familiarity of their subject-matter and the skill of their makers.

SUGGESTED FURTHER READING IN ENGLISH : The standard account of the history of this period is now Jonathan Israel's *The Dutch Republic* (Oxford, 1995). An excellent overview of its artistic production is Seymour Slive's *Dutch Painting 1600–1800* (2nd edition, New Haven and London, 1995). The exhibition catalogue *Masters of 17th-century Dutch Genre Painting* (Royal Academy, London, 1984) and Christopher Brown's *Scenes of Everyday Life* (London, 1984) provide useful introductions to the rich variety of genre painting in this period.

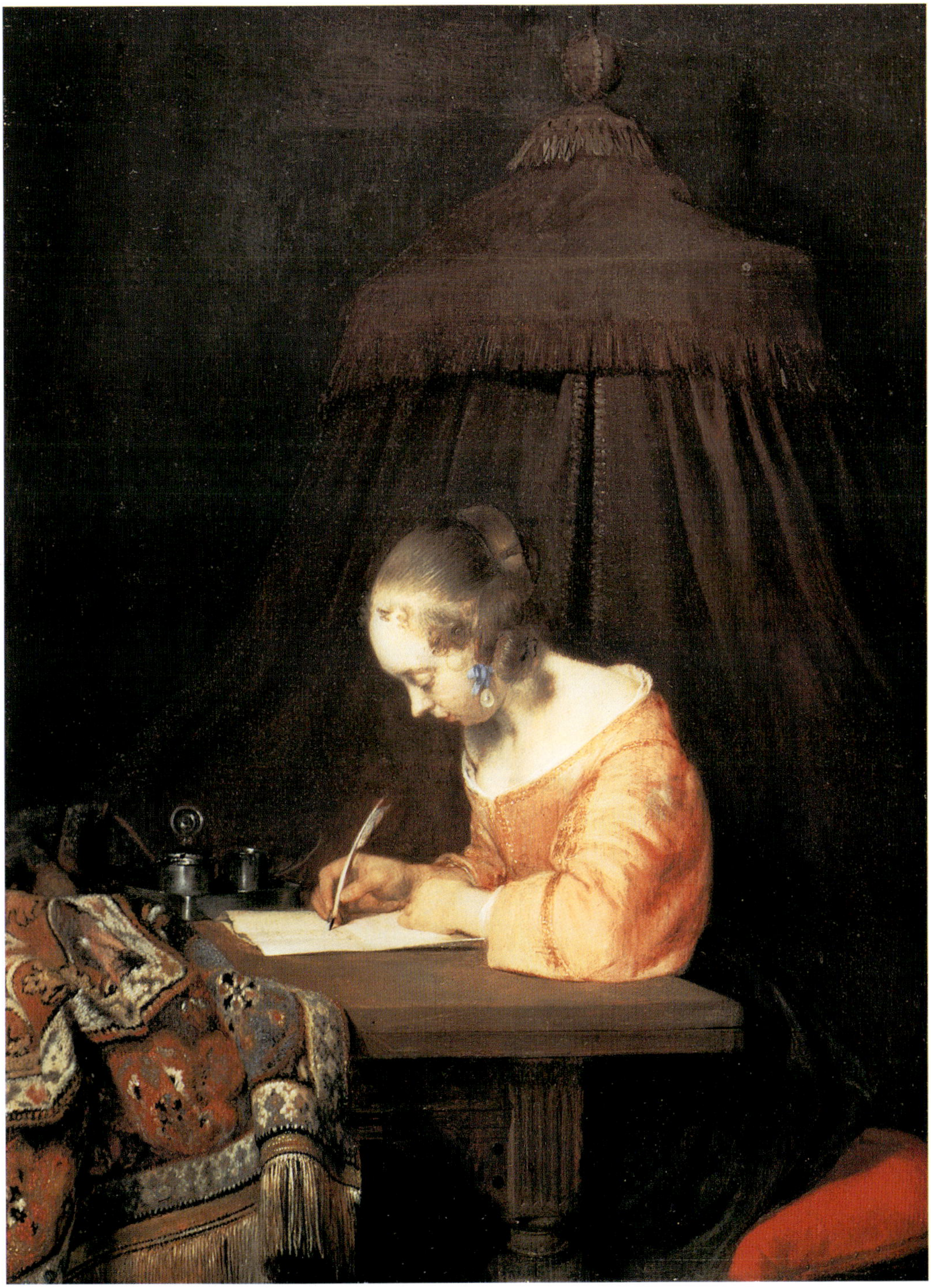

PLATE 18 GERARD TER BORCH : *Woman writing a letter*
Panel, 39 × 29.5 cm. & cover
Signed in monogram : GTB

GERARD TER BORCH (1617–1681)
(PLATES 1 & 18)

He was born in Zwolle and studied there with his father Gerard ter Borch the Elder, who had lived in Italy in his youth. In 1632 Gerard the Younger was in Amsterdam and in 1633 in the studio of the landscape painter Pieter Molijn in Haarlem. He joined the painters' guild in Haarlem, probably in 1635. In that year he went to England and in the late 1630s and 1640s travelled widely in the Netherlands and is said to have visited Germany, Italy, France and Spain. From 1646 until 1648 he was in Münster, painting portraits of the participants in the peace negotiations which were to bring an end to the long war between Spain and the Dutch Republic: he recorded the signing of the peace in his remarkable group portrait *The Swearing of the Oath of Ratification of the Treaty of Münster on the 15th May 1648* (National Gallery, London). In 1653 ter Borch was in Delft but in the following year he married in Deventer, where he was to remain for the rest of his life, becoming a town councillor and in 1667 painting a group portrait of the council, which still hangs in the Town Hall.

Ter Borch's earliest genre scenes are barrack-rooms and interiors in the manner of Codde and Duyster. It was not until the 1650s that he evolved his very distinctive genre painting style, showing richly-dressed figures in elegant, if sparse, interiors. These reveal debts to developments in Delft in the 1650s and so it is fascinating to discover that he was in Delft in 1653. Among ter Borch's pupils was Caspar Netscher.

BIBLIOGRAPHY : The standard catalogue of ter Borch's work is by S. J. Gudlaugsson, *Katalog der Gemälde Gerard ter Borchs*, 2 vols., The Hague, 1960. He was the subject of an exhibition held in the Mauritshuis in 1974, for which there is an excellent catalogue.

PIETER CODDE (1599–1678)

(PLATE 4)

He was born and worked in Amsterdam. In 1637 he completed a large militia group, *The Corporalship of Captain Reynier Reael and Lieutenant Cornelis M. Blaeuw* (Rijksmuseum, Amsterdam), which had been left unfinished by Frans Hals. He was influenced by Hals : his work, which largely consists of small-scale genre paintings showing barrack-rooms, elegant interiors, carnivals and dances, is also close in style to Anthonie Palamedesz. of Delft and Willem Duyster (who may have been his pupil). Codde also painted small-scale portraits with a close attention to detail, especially in dress.

GERRIT DOU (1613–1675)

(PLATE 12)

He was born in Leiden, the son of a glass-engraver and trained in his father's studio. From 1625 until 1627 he was a member of the glaziers' guild, but in 1628 he entered the studio of Rembrandt where he remained until Rembrandt moved to Amsterdam in 1631. Dou rarely left Leiden and was one of the founders of the painters' guild in 1648. One of the most successful of all 17th-century Dutch painters, he had a European reputation. Charles II tried to tempt him to work in England.

Dou was principally a genre painter but also painted small-scale portraits and a few illusionistic still-lifes. His genre scenes, for the most part interiors with figures, are characterised by their high degree of finish and still-life details, which sometimes enrich them with an amorous or vanitas meaning. Dou's earliest training as a glass-engraver can be seen in the miniaturistic technique of his small paintings, which are often on panel. There are many accounts in the early lives of Dou of his painstaking method of painting, which involved working for long hours with the finest of brushes in a dust-free studio. Dou was the founder of the *fijnschilder* School of Leiden. His principal followers, who continued his technique, were Frans Mieris the Elder and Godfried Schalcken. His work was enthusiastically collected not only in his own lifetime but also in 18th-century France and 19th-century England.

BIBLIOGRAPHY : There has been no monographic study of Dou since W. Martin, *Gerrit Dou* (Klassiker der Kunst), Stuttgart/Leipzig, 1913. His work was discussed in the catalogues of exhibitions held in Leiden in 1988 (by Eric Jan Sluijter) and Amsterdam in 1989 (by Peter Hecht). A monographic exhibition will be held in the Dulwich Picture Gallery in 2000.

WILLEM CORNELISZ. DUYSTER (*c.*1599–1635)

(PLATE 5)

He was born in Amsterdam where he may have been a pupil of Pieter Codde (although they were contemporaries). From 1620 his family lived in a house known as De Duystere Werelt (The Dark World) from which they took their name. He lived in Amsterdam painting barrack-room scenes and genre interiors : they are on a small scale with full-length figures in extravagant dress described in great detail and are similar in style to those of Pieter Codde and Simon Kick.

Philip van Dijk (1680–1753)

(PLATE 19)

Van Dijk was born in Amsterdam and was a pupil there of Arnold Boonen. Subsequently he moved to Middelburg and then to The Hague. In 1725 he became court painter to the Landgrave Wilhelm VIII of Hesse in Kassel. Later he returned to The Hague and was appointed court painter to Prince Willem IV of Orange in 1747. He was primarily a portrait painter working in the classicising French style of Nicolaes Maes and Caspar and Constantijn Netscher, making highly finished portraits on a small scale. However, he also painted a number of genre scenes on a similar scale as well as mythological subjects.

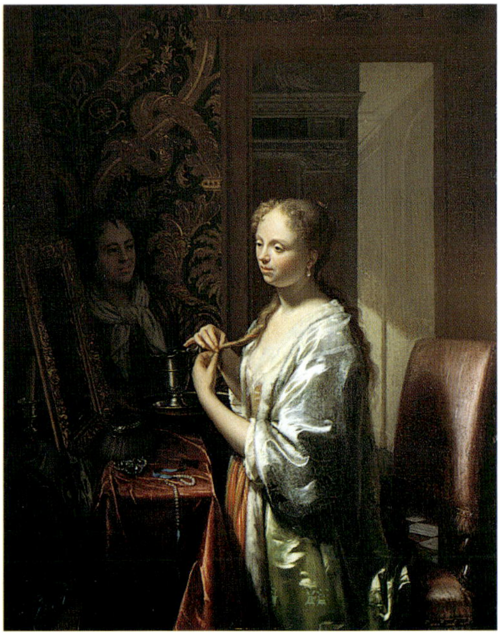

PLATE 19
PHILIP VAN DIJK : *A Lady attending to her toilet*
Panel, 29.5 × 23.5 cm.
Signed : Ph: v. Dijk, F:

Dirk Hals (1591–1656)

(PLATE 3)

He was born in Haarlem, the younger brother of the portrait painter Frans Hals, in whose studio he probably had his first training. He lived and worked in Haarlem but is recorded briefly in Leiden in the 1640s. His style – the forms are created with bold, broad strokes – is based on that of his brother but his subject-matter is exclusively small-scale genre scenes of the 'merry company' type similar to those of Willem Buytewech.

Jacob van Loo (1614–1670)

(PLATE 20)

He was born in Sluis and studied there with his father. He is first recorded in Amsterdam in 1635, where he settled and enjoyed great success. With Gerbrandt van den Eeckhout he created a new type of interior scene with elegant dressed figures music-making, flirting, eating and drinking in richly appointed settings. They reflect the prosperous style of life of contemporary Amsterdammers. Van Loo also received important commissions from the Prince of Orange. In 1670, having been involved in a fight, he fled from Amsterdam to Paris, where he worked for the rest of his life.

Nicolaes Maes (1634–93)

(PLATE 16)

He was born in Dordrecht and was a pupil in Rembrandt's Amsterdam studio around 1650. He was back in Dordrecht in 1653 and remained there until 1673 when he moved to Amsterdam. For a short time after his return from Rembrandt's studio Maes painted domestic interiors which are characterised by a rich chiaroscuro and a precise treatment of still-life detail : both in style and subject-matter they reveal

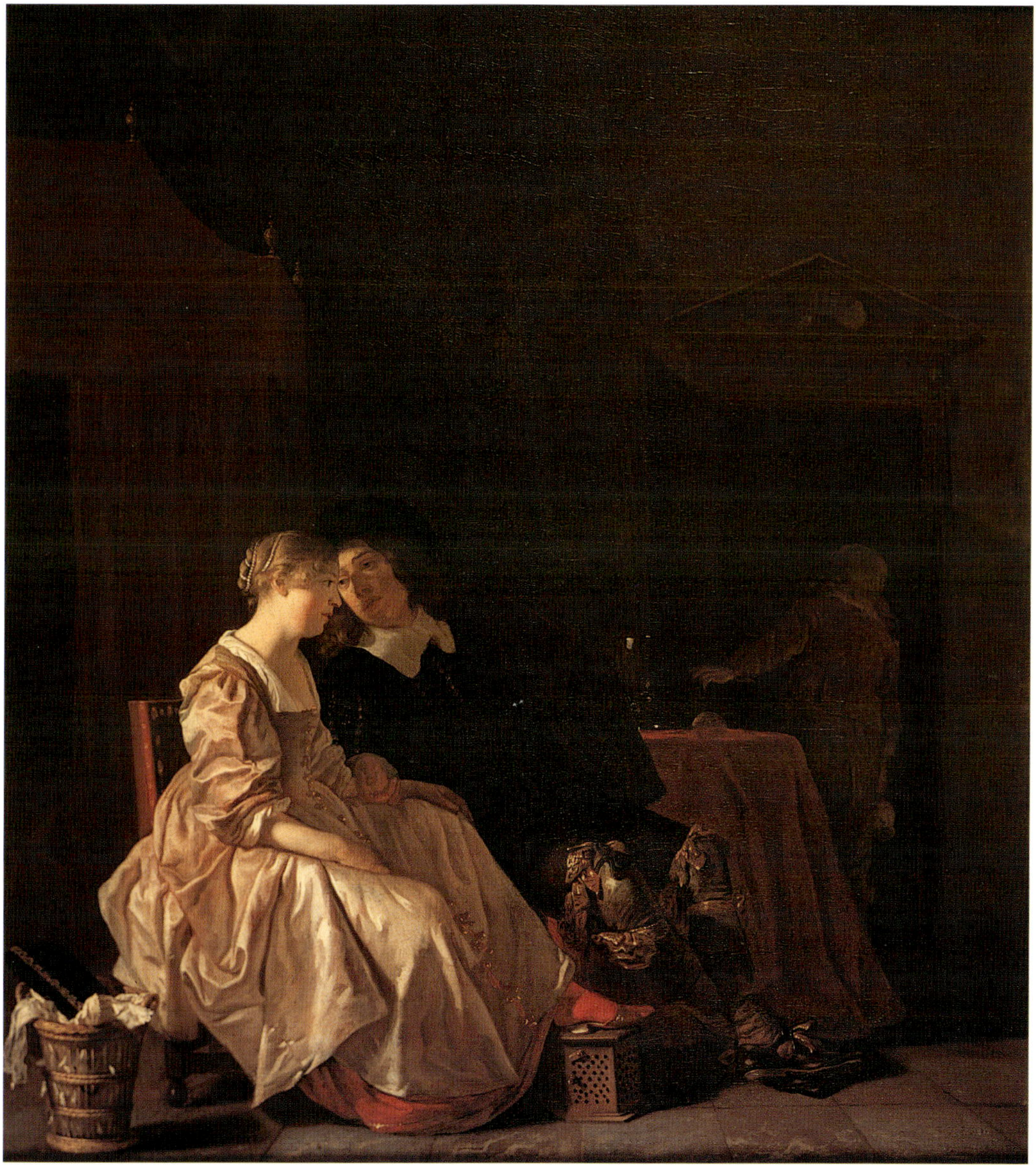

PLATE 20
JACOB VAN LOO : *Wooing* Canvas, 73.3 × 66.8 cm.

fascinating similarities to contemporary developments in Delft (particularly in the work of Carel Fabritius and Pieter de Hooch). After 1660 Maes devoted himself to portraiture, painting small-scale, bust-length portraits which were in great demand and display the influence of Anthony van Dyck.

GABRIEL METSU (1629–1667)

(PLATE 15)

Born in Leiden, he was the son of a Flemish painter who had settled in the town. He was a pupil of his father and, probably, of Gerrit Dou. He was a founder member of the new Leiden guild in 1648 but by 1657 had moved

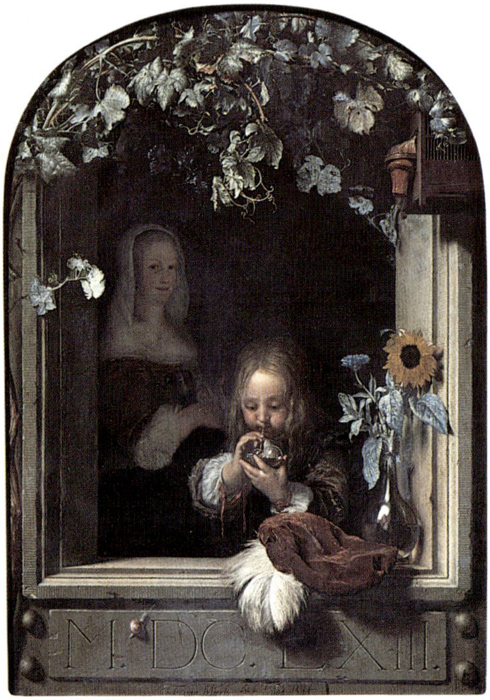

PLATE 21

FRANS VAN MIERIS THE ELDER : *A Boy blowing bubbles*

Panel, 25.5 × 19 cm.

Signed and dated : M.DC.LXIII.[1663] F. van Mieris. fect. Lugd. Bat

A child – in the 16th century a *putto*, in the 17th century a child in contemporary dress – blowing a bubble is a familiar symbol of *vanitas* in Dutch genre painting. Since classical times the fragility of man's life has been compared to a soap bubble. Van Mieris is deliberately referring to this *homo bulla* (man as a soap bubble) tradition in this scene which at first simply appears to show the carefree activities of childhood.

to Amsterdam, where he remained until his death. Metsu's subject-matter is eclectic, pointing to the influence of Dou, Steen, ter Borch, de Hooch and others, but his exquisite, refined technique, particularly in the description of texture, is highly original. In addition to his many genre paintings of interiors and street and market scenes, Metsu also painted a number of religious subjects and still-lifes.

BIBLIOGRAPHY : F.W. Robinson, Gabriel Metsu : *A Study of his Place in the Genre Painting of the Golden Age*, New York, 1974.

FRANS VAN MIERIS THE ELDER (1635–1681)

(PLATES 13 & 21)

He was born in Leiden, the son of a goldsmith and the pupil of a glass-painter and then of Dou, who is said to have called Van Mieris "the Prince of my Pupils". Like Dou, Van Mieris had a European reputation but although he received commissions from Archduke Leopold and Cosimo III of Tuscany, he rarely left Leiden. He was a leading member of the Leiden school of *fijnschilders*, who followed Dou in the high degree of finish in their paintings. As well as genre scenes, he painted portraits and religious, classical, literary and allegorical subjects. Van Mieris was imitated by his sons, Jan and Willem, and by his grandson, Frans the Younger, who carried the family tradition into the second half of the 18th century.

BIBLIOGRAPHY : O. Naumann, *Frans van Mieris the Elder*, 2 vols., Doornspijk, 1981.

JAN MIENSE MOLENAER (*c.*1610–1668)

(PLATES 7–11)

He was born in Haarlem and was probably a pupil there of Frans Hals. His earliest work is from 1629. In 1636 he married Judith Leyster, who had been in Hals' studio and in the following year they were living in Amsterdam. In 1648 they returned to Heemstede, near Haarlem. His paintings are almost all of genre subjects (some with significant allegorical elements) painted in the broad manner of Hals. Later he painted

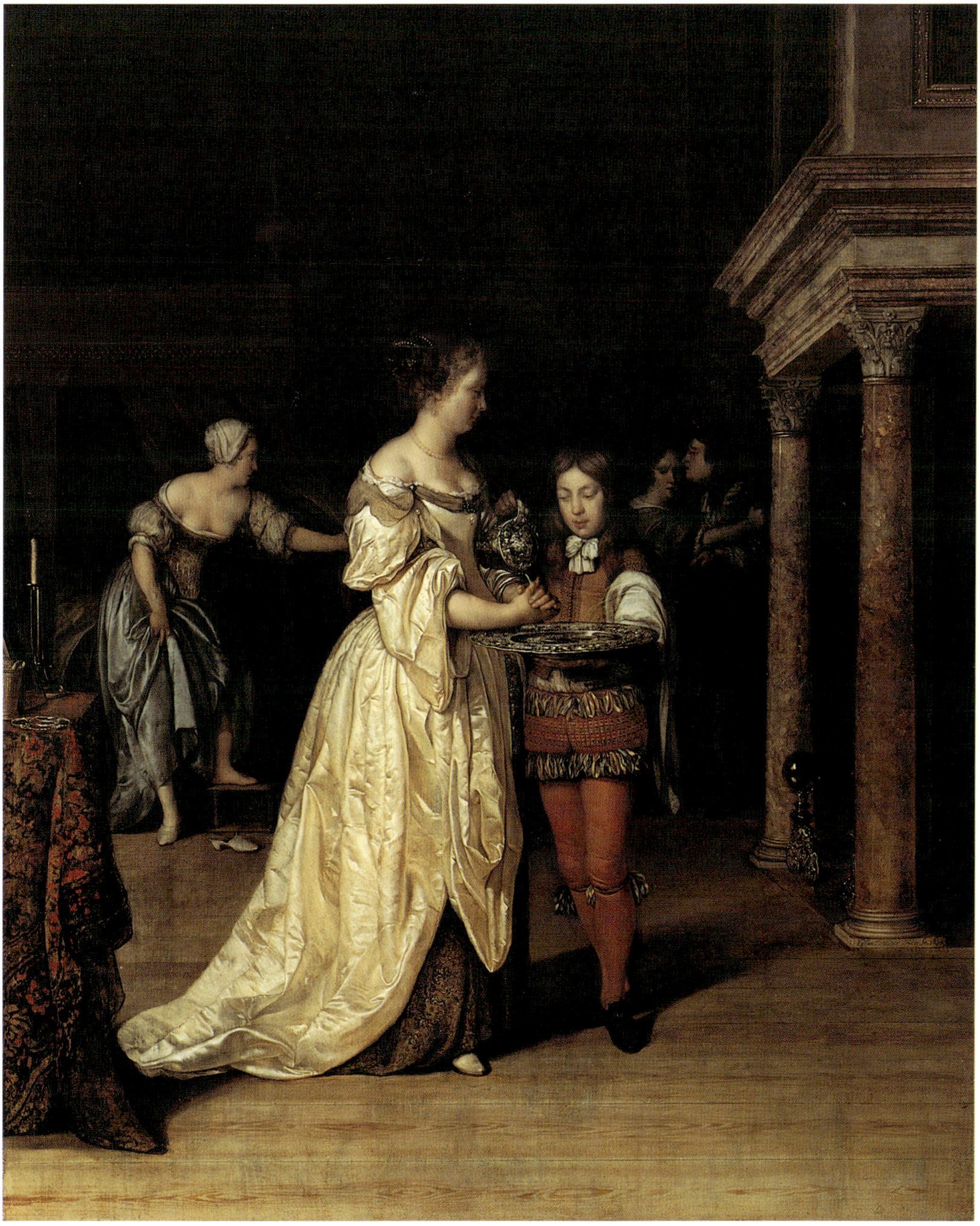

PLATE 22

EGLON VAN DER NEER : *Interior with a woman washing her hands*
Panel, 49 × 39.5 cm.
Signed and dated : Eglon vander Neer 1675

a number of peasant interiors in a style which reveals his study of Adriaen van Ostade.

Eglon van der Neer (*c*.1634–1703)

(plate 22)

He was born in Amsterdam and studied with his father the moonlight and winter landscape painter, Aert van der Neer. He moved a great deal, working in Rotterdam, The Hague and Brussels as well as Amsterdam. His final move was to Dusseldorf, where he was court painter to the Elector Palatine, Johan Wilhelm. In addition to his elegant and highly refined interiors, he painted religious and classical subjects, portraits and landscapes. Adriaen van der Werff was his pupil.

Jacob Ochtervelt (1634–1682)

(plate 6)

He was born in Rotterdam and is said to have been a pupil of the landscape painter Nicolaes Berchem in Haarlem. He returned to Rotterdam and remained there until 1674, when he moved to Amsterdam. He painted domestic interiors based on the houses of the wealthier residents of Rotterdam and Amsterdam. His rooms scarcely hold more than one or two figures, often rather schematically treated, with an acute feeling for their precise placing and the rich fabrics of their clothes. He also painted a few portraits and, in his earliest years, landscapes.

bibliography : S. Kuretsky, *The Paintings of Jacob Ochtervelt*, Oxford, 1979.

Adriaen van Ostade (1610–1685)

(plate 2)

He was born in Haarlem and was a pupil there of Frans Hals at the same time as the Flemish painter of peasant scenes, Adriaen Brouwer. He remained in Haarlem, where he enjoyed considerable success. He painted, etched and drew scenes of peasant life and his early style reflects the powerful influence of Brouwer. He was remarkably prolific : more than 800 paintings, over fifty etchings and several hundred drawings and watercolours survive. He also painted a few Biblical subjects and several portraits. Among his pupils were his younger brother Isack, Cornelis Dusart and Cornelis Bega.

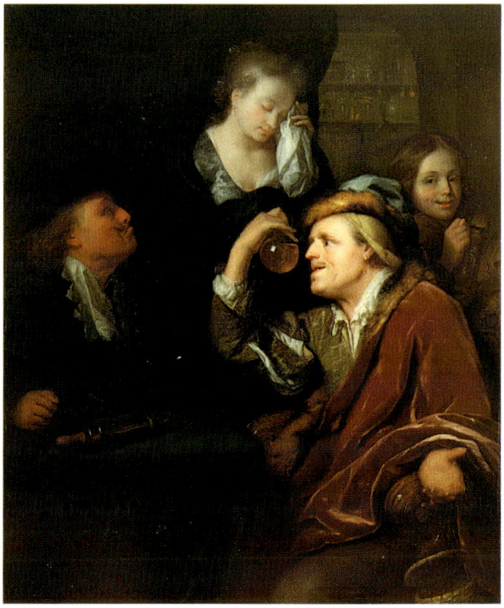

plate 23
Godfried Schalcken : *The medical examination*
Panel, 35 × 28.5 cm.
Signed : G. Schalcken

Godfried Schalcken (1643–1706)

(plates 14 & 15)

He was born near Dordrecht and was a pupil there of Samuel van Hoogstraten. He later trained with Gerrit Dou in Leiden. He was back in Dordrecht by 1665 and remained there until 1691. He travelled to England in the following year and stayed until 1698, during which time he painted several

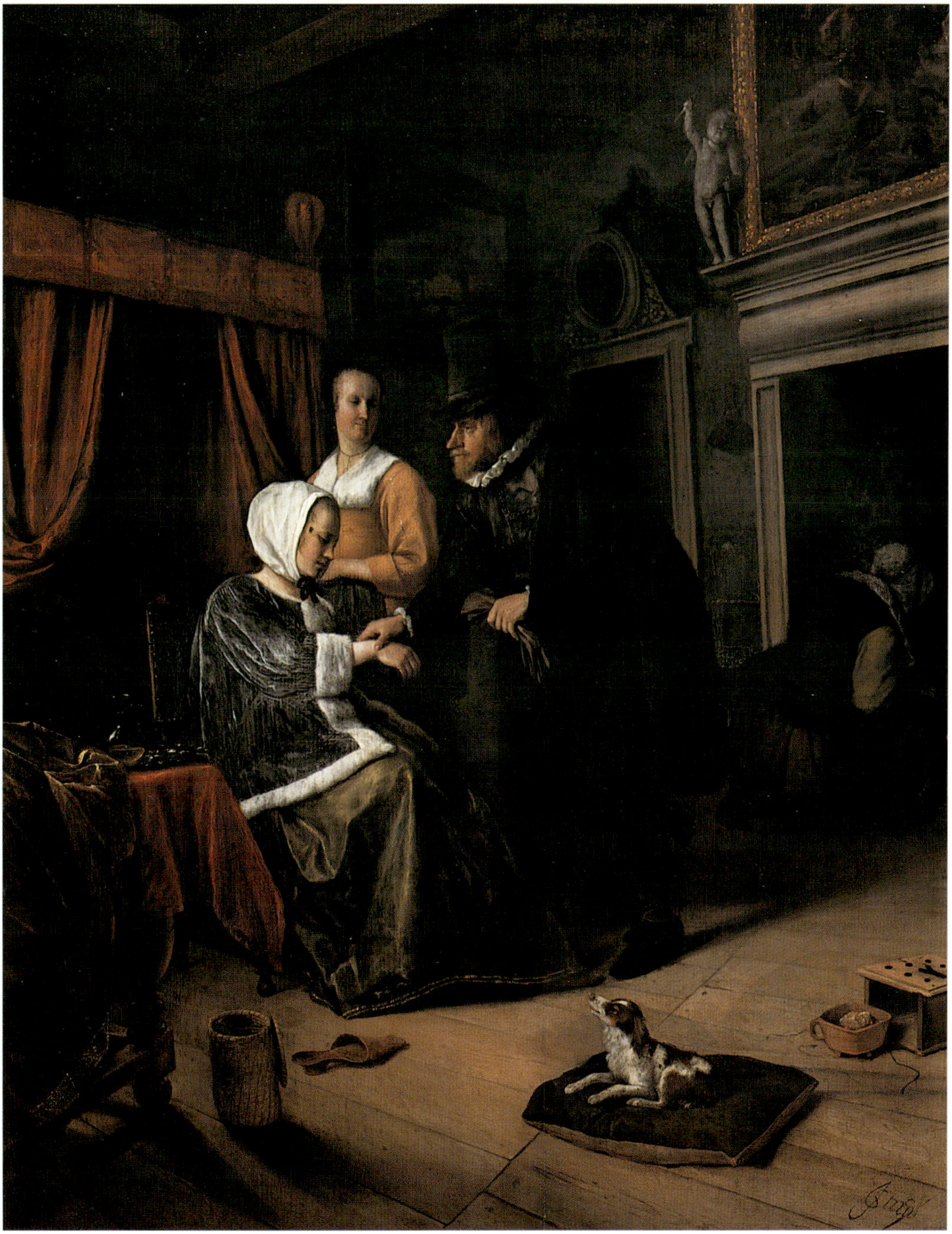

PLATE 24 JAN STEEN : *The sick girl*
Panel, 58 × 46.5 cm.
Signed : Jsteen

The young woman is suffering from 'love's sickness', that is, she is pregnant. The ribbon burning in the earthenware vessel in the foreground is a reference to a folk method of determining pregnancy. The cupid on the mantelpiece also refers to the young woman's predicament.

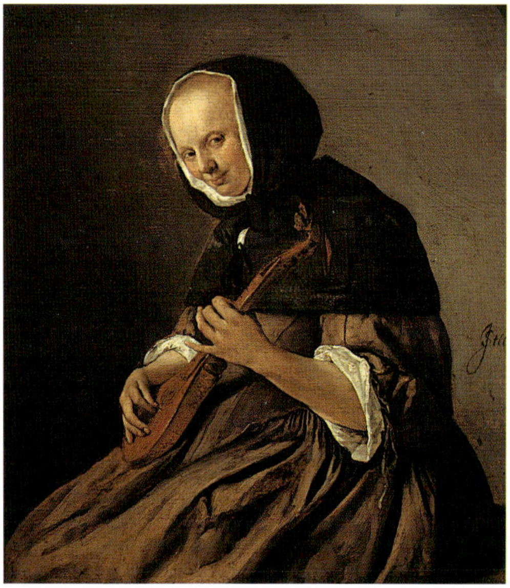

PLATE 25
JAN STEEN : *Woman playing the sistrum*
Panel, 31 × 27.5 cm
Signed : Jsteen

Traditionally the sitter has been identified as the painter's wife (and daughter of his teacher) Grietje van Goyen. She plays a *sistrum*, a miniature lute.

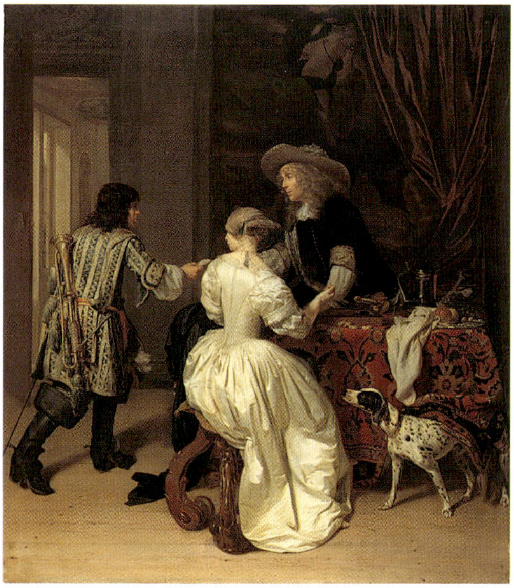

PLATE 26
JAN VERKOLJE : *The messenger*
Canvas, 59 × 53.5 cm.
Signed and dated : I. Verkolje 1674

portraits of King William III. His remaining years were spent in The Hague and Dusseldorf, where he worked for the Elector Palatine, Johann Wilhelm. Schalcken was very successful, enjoying a European reputation during his lifetime, particularly with *fijnschilder* genre scenes shown by artificial light and small-scale portraits (some of which are also illuminated by candle-light). His early style owes much to Dou. He also painted religious and mythological subjects as well as a few allegorical and literary ones.

JAN STEEN (1625/6–1679)

(PLATES 17, 24 & 25)

He was born in Leiden but is said to have trained with Adriaen van Ostade in Haarlem and Jan van Goyen (whose daughter he married) in The Hague. He joined the guild in Leiden in 1648 but also worked in The Hague and in Delft. Subsequently he lived in Warmond, near Leiden, and then in Haarlem. Finally he returned to Leiden in the mid-1660s and spent the remaining years of his life there, serving as an officer in the guild in the 1670s. A prolific painter, Steen concentrated on lively genre scenes but also painted portraits and religious and mythological subjects. His work, which is markedly uneven in quality, is characterised by a robust humour and a strong sense of theatre.

BIBLIOGRAPHY : The catalogue of the Jan Steen exhibition held at the National Gallery of Art, Washington and the Rijksmuseum in 1996 : *Jan Steen, Painter and Storyteller* is the most up-to-date account of the artist.

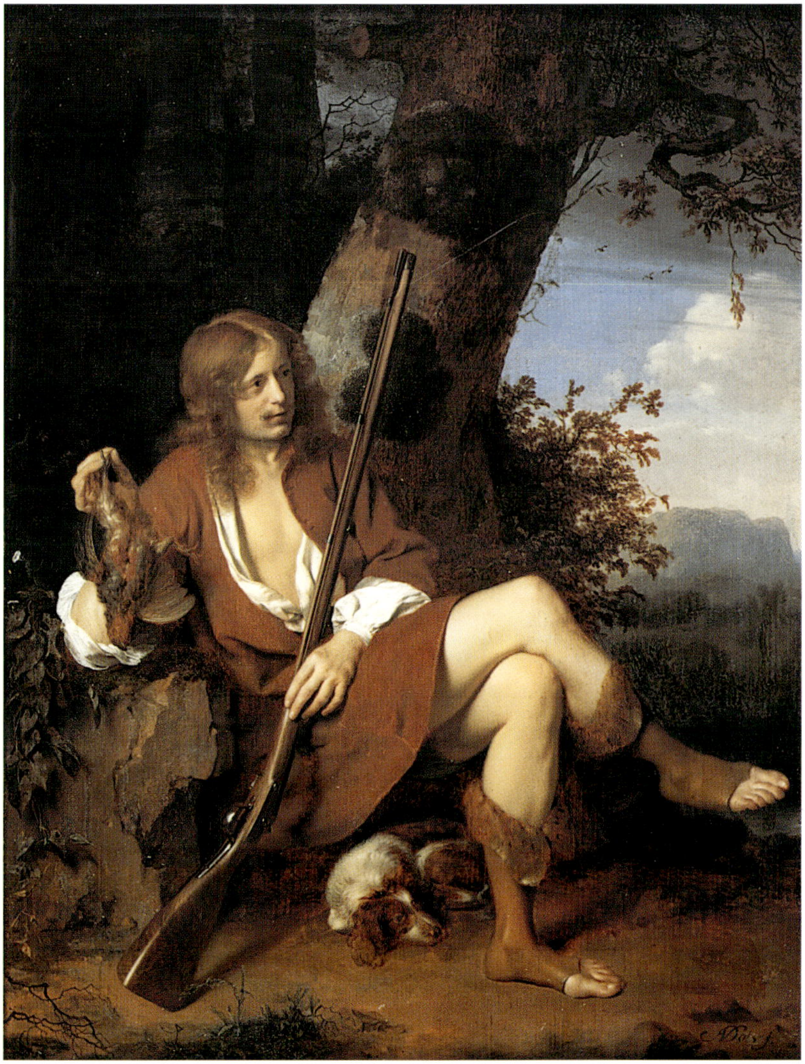

PLATE 27
ARIE DE VOIS:
Self-portrait as a hunter
Panel, 29 × 22 cm.
Signed: ADVois f.

JAN VERKOLJE (1650–1693)

(PLATE 26)

He was born in Amsterdam and is said to have studied with Jan Andries Lievens. He moved to Delft and entered the guild there in 1673. He served as a guild officer between 1678 and 1688 and died in the town. He painted mythological scenes and portraits as well as scenes of elegant figures in richly appointed interiors.

ARIE DE VOIS (*c.*1632–1680)

(PLATE 27)

Born in Utrecht into a family of musicians. When he was a child the family moved to Leiden. He is said to have trained with Nicolaes Knupfer in Utrecht and Abraham van den Tempel in Leiden. He joined the Leiden guild in 1653 and served as an officer during the 1660s. He worked in the Leiden tradition of the *fijnschilders*, painting genre scenes as well as portraits and classical subjects.

PAINTINGS

(in alphabetical order of artists)

GERRIT BERCKHEYDE : *The Hofvijver in The Hague with a view of the Mauritshuis*
PREFACE
Canvas, 58 × 68.5 cm.
Signed : gerret: Berck Heijde

GERARD TER BORCH : *Unwelcome News*
PLATE 1
Panel, 66.7 × 59.5 cm.
Signed, GTB (in monogram) 1653

GERARD TER BORCH : *Woman writing a letter*
PLATE 18
Panel, 39 × 29.5 cm. & cover
Signed in monogram : GTB

PIETER CODDE : *Festivity with masked dancers*
PLATE 4
Panel, 50 × 76.5 cm.
Signed and dated : Pcodde Ao 1636

GERARD DOU : *Young woman holding a lamp*
PLATE 12
Panel, 19 × 14 cm.

WILLEM CORNELISZ. DUYSTER : *An Officer*
PLATE 5
Panel, 40 × 31.5 cm.

PHILIP VAN DIJK : *A Lady attending to her toilet*
PLATE 19
Panel, 29.5 × 23.5 cm.
Signed : Ph: v. Dijk, F:

DIRK HALS : *Merry Company*
PLATE 3
Panel, 30 × 51.5 cm.
Signed and dated : D Hals 1635

JACOB VAN LOO : *Wooing*
PLATE 20
Canvas, 73.3 × 66.8 cm.

NICOLAES MAES : *The Old Lace-maker*
PLATE 16
Canvas, 37.5 × 35 cm.

GABRIEL METSU : *A Young Woman composing music*
PLATE 15
Panel, 57.8 × 43.5 cm.
Signed : G Metsu

FRANS VAN MIERIS THE ELDER : *A Boy blowing bubbles*
PLATE 21
Panel, 25.5 × 19 cm.
Signed and dated : M.DC.LXIII.[1663] F. van Mieris. fect. Lugd. Bat

FRANS VAN MIERIS THE ELDER : *Teasing the pet*
PLATE 13
Panel, 27.5 × 20 cm.
Signed and dated : Fv Mieris Ao 1660

JAN MIENSE MOLENAER : *The Five Senses : Touch*
PLATE 7
Panel, 19.5 × 24.2 cm.
Signed and dated : IMR 1637

JAN MIENSE MOLENAER : *The Five Senses : Sight*
PLATE 8
Panel, 19.6 × 23.9 cm.
Signed : IMR

JAN MIENSE MOLENAER : *The Five Senses : Sound*
PLATE 9
Panel, 19.4 × 24.2 cm.

JAN MIENSE MOLENAER : *The Five Senses : Smell*
PLATE 10
Panel, 19.5 × 24.3 cm.

JAN MIENSE MOLENAER : *The Five Senses : Taste*
PLATE 11
Panel, 19.6 × 24.1 cm.

EGLON VAN DER NEER : *Interior with a woman washing her hands*
PLATE 22
Panel, 49 × 39.5 cm.
Signed and dated : Eglon vander Neer 1675

JACOB OCHTERVELT : *The Fishmonger*
PLATE 6
Canvas, 55.5 × 44 cm.

ADRIAEN VAN OSTADE : *Peasants in an Inn*
PLATE 2
Panel, 47 × 39 cm.
Signed and dated : Av. Ostade 1662

GODFRIED SCHALCKEN : *The wasted lesson in morals*
PLATE 14
Panel, 35 × 28.5 cm.
Signed : G. Schalcken

GODFRIED SCHALCKEN : *The medical examination*
PLATE 23
Panel, 35 × 28.5 cm.
Signed : G. Schalcken

JAN STEEN : *The sick girl*
PLATE 24
Panel, 58 × 46.5 cm.
Signed : Jsteen

JAN STEEN : *Girl eating oysters*
PLATE 17
Panel, 20.5 × 14.5 cm.
Signed : IS

JAN STEEN : *Woman playing the sistrum*
PLATE 25
Panel, 31 × 27.5 cm
Signed : Jsteen

JAN VERKOLJE : *The messenger*
PLATE 26
Canvas, 59 × 53.5 cm.
Signed and dated : I. Verkolje 1674

ARIE DE VOIS : *Self-portrait as a hunter*
PLATE 27
Panel, 29 × 22 cm.
Signed : ADVois f.